# Les Chansons de la Vie

## Natalie Cheng

BookLeaf Publishing

Presentation by *BookLeaf Publishing*

Web: www.bookleafpub.com

E-mail: info@bookleafpub.com

ISBN: 9789395756181

First edition 2022

The first time I met the sea
I brushed his tension with my eyes;
He caressed my curves with his breath
And loved me wild and wet.

The first time I met the mountain
He raised me on his back;
With sculpted body he supported me
Steadfast and true.

The first time I met the sky
He courted my soul and set it ablaze,
Crowning an aura on his beloved.

The first time I met her I asked for Forgiveness;
I pulled her from Untouchable hell,
Washed her,
And held her hand.

Broken and wounded,
We united our hearts
As one.

When I met the stars,
I shot an emboldened wish
For peace and to be loved,
As I embrace the journey ahead.

# — Lost and Found

Last night a comet came before me;
He carried a box and asked for my wish;
"Anything" he said,
"I'll send it to the wish granters".

Without hesitation
I knew what I wanted.
I grabbed the box and whispered my deepest
Desire.

With a nod he departed and flew away;
Sprinkling the letters that I've kept hidden from
your ears
Into the twilight.

Tonight I breathed it into the night;
So perhaps you'd feel my heart
As the moonlight kisses your cheek
And whispers,
"I love you".

— Admirer

Your folded clothes are next to my knees
Grazing the forbidden space between us.
Static teases the distance we placed between us.
Electricity dares to challenge
Convention's physics.
Drawing me in.


I look up and our dirty towels
Hang from the rack.
Clinging to the memories of the morning, daring
us to reignite the watery fire.
The pure explosion of fireworks that
Coursed through the air.


Your voice echoes in our small room,
A reminder of home.
Safety in wild oblivion.
When heaven is aflame in
Passion and peace.


Your deepest notes tattooed on my heart .
I breathe in your air,
Inhaling the baritone oxygen that
Harmonizes with my soul

Untitled and new, we plunge into the future
Together but apart.
Beauty has never touched me like this.
We resurrect each other from
Mediocrity and discover
A colourful rebirth

— Sunday Morning

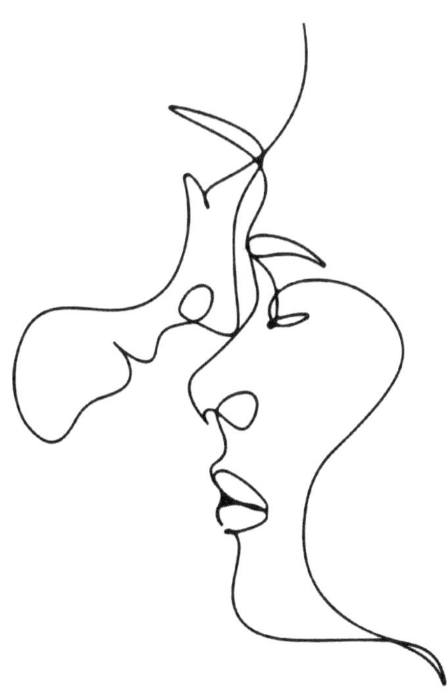

My love is blind;
He cannot see me so I let him feel me
So he can see me.

My love is blind;
He cannot hear me so I let him kiss me
So he can taste my love.

My love is blind;
He does not know me so I let him in
So he won't forget my soul

My love is blind;
His eyes never dove into the depths of mine;
My devotions were unknown.

In vain have I loved you;
In pain do I unlove you
And yet I miss you as you go out the door.

— Crush

Overthinking the future;
Overposting the present;
Overanalyzing the past;
Oversharing my thoughts;
Overstimulated mind;
Overcrowded with tasks;

Staring at the white stone sky...
Frozen.
Thirsting for a cure.

— Anticipation Paralysis

How do I describe the pain of losing you?
No of leaving us behind;
Leaving you behind;
Leaving you ahead;
I don't know anymore.


It's sitting in a deserted airport
remembering the safety of your shoulders;
It's seeing your face in the crowd;
It's hearing your voice in empty halls;
It's feeling your heart when I see a similar soul;
It's taking a double take thinking …maybe..
You're here with me.


Now
It is constant pain, the kind that is so clear
It's hidden;
Like a glass dagger
Stabbing and twisting my heart.


It is screaming to the universe to reverse it,
To bring you back;
That I was wrong;
That this isn't real.

It is surrendering,
Knowing it was for the best
That we existed as opposites;
Never to attract.


And I am cursed with the gift of breaking the
One I love.


— Gone

Bliss was the life I had with you;
Paradise was the home you made;
Steadfast were you standing by me;
Peace was your touch;
Safe was your hand in mine;
Joy was you
You…
You…


You're here!
No longer remembering but living.
We are together, Baby stay!
It's going to be okay!
My mind follows the specter off the cliff
About to jump
Into Limbo


No!!
A hand thrusts me back to reality;
I fight
I scream,
Please!
Don't take me back!
I'd rather be insane
Than live in the shadows of lost time.

Helpless,
I give up.
I am drunk,
Intoxicated by the mirage
Of an evaporated love;
Smoking the fumes of a dying dream.


— Delusional

In the night I hide from a violent lover;
And plan for escape;
In fear, I ration my energies.

Ambushed, I remember you;
The man who dove into hell for the one heaven
rejected
And carried her through Calvary;
Breathed love into my lungs;
And revived my broken soul.

I remember your kindness;
Your gentle touch;
I remember how I we took on the world;
How I glowed next to you.

A fool,
I have given love where love was not due.
You are my shooting star;
My best friend.
And if I die here from unkind hands,
My naïve heart will be grateful to have loved
And been loved by you.

— Goodbye

I wish you knew

How my heart beats for you when you're not
around;
How I wonder how you're doing 3 hours away;
How I long to be with you;
How I miss your voice in my ear.

I wish you were

Here


— Present


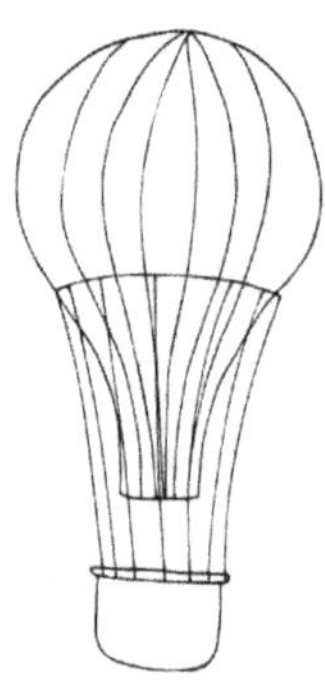

From the depths I rise,
Defiant.
I've visited hell and looked the Devil in the eye;
Burnt and Untamed,
I rise from the ashes and reach up.

A hand holds me;
Pulls me up;
My wings erupt from my shoulders,
they're bloody and new;
With the feather weight I fly,
Leaving the nest.

Jackles eat at my heels;
I fight them off,
losing my legs;
I cannot walk;
Lighter I soar.

And as I weep, a rainbow follows me;
I pave the unbeaten path
For a strong, empowered woman.

— Tomorrow

Biblical carnage;
Hemorrhaging agape;
She arose from faded canvas with
Renewed definition;
I am branded with my colours;
Freeing my caged soul.

— Blossoming

I walk my life in mist and grey,
Paving paths of concrete to feel the ground;
Chained to the roads,
I walk as I should.

The storms come and the flood roars,
Ripping the shackles;
I am lost in the waves
And my eyes rest in the skies.

In the chaos I transform;
My legs become fins and
I dance the water song;
I am lost in Ocean blues.

My tears rest in the sea,
I am found in your eyes;
Asleep are my inequities,
Awakened is my strength.

I will not look back,
I will not live what's died;
Only to live by your love
I emerge a freed one.

— Brother

I had an older sister who died before she lived.

My mother would tell me about how she flew
Home too soon.

Sometimes I wonder if she sees me with her
Unopened eyes when I'm not sure how to be.

Sometimes I wished her voice to life to guide
My wounded self out of the nightmares.

Yesterday I dreamed a vision.
She took my hand and embraced my tired heart.

Today I met her only to fly away and love her
From afar.

                                        — Sister

When you find someone
Whose eyes meet yours;
Whose heart hears yours;
Whose body fits yours;
Whose spirit blesses yours;
Whose tongue speaks yours;
Whose mind ignites yours;
Whose presence honours yours;
Only to leave them the next day
hundreds of miles away,
To live worlds apart;
Wishing to find home again.

— Homeless

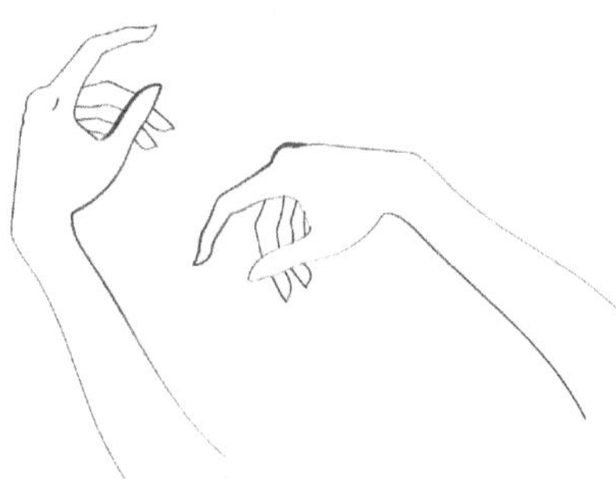

Painted by chivalry chosen;
Sculpted by kindness and strength;
Saltiness retained;
Sweetness aged;
A lion, dangerous and untamed,
Generous in intention,
And introspective in name
Is the one I seek;
A harmonious chaos
Of fire and water
To be mine
And I, his.

— Lover

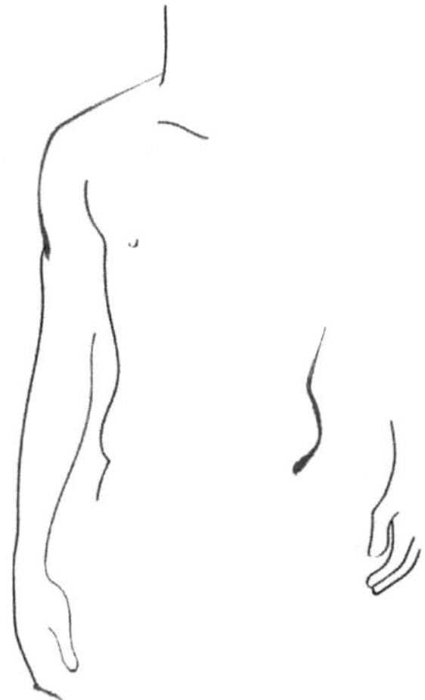

My mind has found its worthy opponent,
My heart has found its keeper,
My hands have met their match,
And my soul has met its kin.

If only you weren't so far away,
If only I had stayed one more day,
If only we were both free;
For it is inopportune for me to love you
And yet I have fallen for you
in the 32 hours, I knew you.

Now at the crossroads, I stay;
Unable to walk away from you;
Although reason pushes my feet
My heart holds me still;
Looking back to find your face
One last time
Looking for a reason to stay.

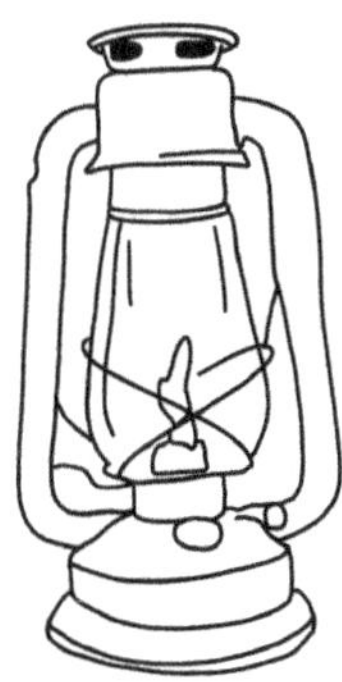

— Mr. Thirty-two

It is said that lovers live amongst the stars;
Immortalized in the cosmos
As tragic inspirations.

Stripped of their bodies,
Their souls lie bare and bright
In Pangeal nostalgia.

It starts with collisions;
Starcrossed and untimely;
Scientifically improbable
Two souls meet;
A mortal engagement

An oration of intrigue,
Their lips dance in distanced complexity
As words spin the rope that ties
the Knot;
Enchanted, I fall into your gravity.

Your smile undresses me
And my boundaries happily fall away;
The undoing of my binding cloth
That's hidden the access to my heart

Naked before you, my soul dances and sings;
I welcome your gaze and reach for your hands;
Bare Chested, I bare my heart;
Vulnerable.

Daring you to leave.

Requited, you caress me and behold my curves;
A dangerous tango of undoable impermanence;
Wild and fickle,
Our lives collide and erupt in wild flames;
Lighting up the night.

Our story is etched in the universe;
A tragedy sewn in the sky;
Starcrossed and doomed,
An erotic tease.

The clock strikes twelve
And we say goodbye;
With your leave,
My dream dies
And you take a part
Of who I am
As I find you in the stars.

— Unrequited

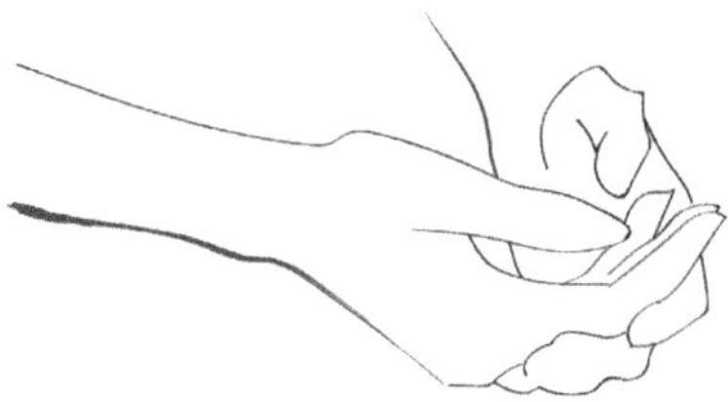

I gave all I had to porous hands;
No one knew
How to hold me.

I stood before you weak and hungry
With hands
Grasping for air.

Your fingers breathed into mine,
Weaving the dance
That birthed my laughter.

You gave me spirit and newness
In food and drink;
I wanted to live again.

We moved as one in spiritual rhythm;
You held me
And my soul rested.

My days were numbered
But you sacrificed your rest
To honour our time
Until we return to nothingness
As we were before.

— Provider

I registered for a hungered game
They say that its rewards have held
Men ransom to their dreams;
Doomed to delusion.


Strong and defiant,
I have armoured myself with mined steel
and iron blades;
Impenetrable, I march forth.


But they did not warn me of you
With a feather, you cut my defenses;
Enamoured and dazed,
I struggled to stand.


Cupid, thou art a shrewd beast.
To kill what life I had left and give it to
My captor;
Powerless, I surrender.


Alone, you left me.
After taking everything I had;
After toying with my puppet strings;
I stare at the sky and weep.

Empty, I stood
A shell of what I was before;
I brush off the dirt and let myself bleed,
As I walk on


— Resilience

I used to hate
What is now beloved.
This body's
Sinew and strength
Are synonymous with beauty.
I behold myself with new eyes
And become a new
Woman.


— Beyoncé

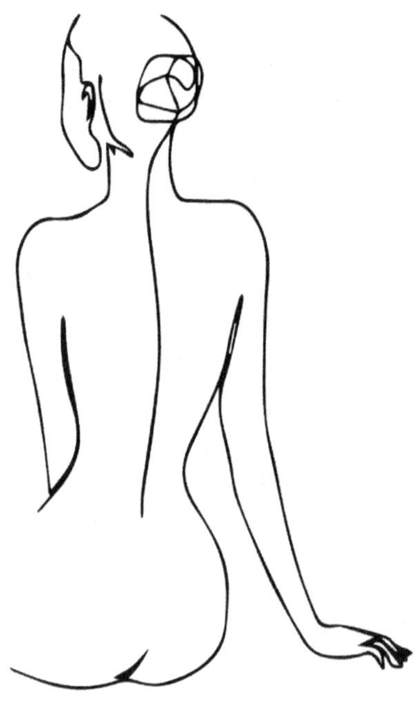

Space is often feared
The need to satisfy and serve
To fill the air with words and action


Space is often sought
To breathe
To hide in
A precious space to let the past pass and die


One day a man welcomed me into his space;
shared.
Come, he motioned
Take up space he said
Freely I see you
And freely I give you...


Space for your weakness
Space for your strengths
Space for your fears
Space for your words


I am here

Breathing in the silence, I am
Engulfed with the air that revives my peace
Holy is the space that welcomes a person to
Enter as they are


Ominous and powerful is the space that is
Shared
For in the break of time you made for me,
You've broken the stranger and
Forged a friend


— Seen

I met him,
Pressed for time,
Running at 100 beats to stay alive.

In the seconds I paused,
He jumpstarted my core,
200 joules worth.

Electric, his hands tickled my skin
And in the moonlight,
Two pilgrims meet.

In asystolic bliss
My cheeks burn and I smile
As my heart danced again

— Defibrillated

The candle cannot be covered,
Its light burns through its covers;
It ignites with passion and spreads;
Refusing to be ignored.

To speak your name is to summon
A Lion.
You are unmatched in valour;
And your legacy is endless.

For one who loves with such fiery
Is one who will be remembered.

— Unforgettable

Two comets flying to converge
And collide in a star crossed explosion
Fireworks
We met in unexpected circumstance
A short lived dreamy
Romance
And now as we part, I stand tall
Shining in the stigmata of a past lover
Whose kiss sent me into
Oblivion

— Starstruck

In shadows of missed time I
Curse the moments reserved.

The sun scorches me;
He mocks me with false light.

I walk quickly, trying to outrun time;
Racing to meet the night

And forget the today that never was.

— Sunburnt

My heart has taken a pilgrimage that
Does not exist;

On unholy ground she trods in search of
The one she loves.

But she labours in vain.
She cries and sees that she is lost.

Left behind, I take her hand and lead her away
From a story that never was

— Heartbroken

I walk on the street;
So much noise;
People talking, people laughing
At me,
With me.

I walk off the earth;
Who will follow me?
No one shares the things I see;
The fall is insidious
and suddenly,
I fly.

I walk to the moon;
A little prince joins me
And we finally find peace.
In this joy
I wonder,

Will you miss me when I'm gone?

— Miss Me

Since birth I thought in colour,
Metaphors and song;
My heart spoke its truth
That fell on deaf ears.


Silvertongues engulfed me;
I learned quickly to be
Multilingual;
The chameleon's gift.


I adapted, adopted, adjusted;
Additions of logics and tactics;
Fighting illiteracy with
Forced camoflauge.


Twenty years later, I won with
Marked success;
No longer the runt of the litter
Suffocating my voice to be
Seen.

But no one saw
Me.
My identity falsified and future threatened;
My heart wasted away
Into a walking corpse;
A Silvertongue.


One day, they orphaned
The imposter;
They left her to burn in righteous fire;
They discarded and broke
Her shameful being.


In an endless beating she learned
Helplessness;
In her darkest hour
You were out of sight and mind
For your convenience.


Indignant, her wounds roared and
Through cracked silver
Her colours bled,
Flooding the thrown flames;
Combusting the world in fire and fury.

As the ashes set
She rose in red plumage;
Claiming her throne in the heavens.


Challenging her captors,
She threatening to breathe
Her truth,


"Golden are my lips
Hardened and sharp
As I speak my golden tongue
And leave The hyenas behind"


—— Noncompliance

In his cave I studied the shadows
Of beings that promised the world;
I watched as the figures danced and
Disappeared,
Wondering who was behind these
Confused illusions.


Dangerous, they warned me, were my
Thoughts;
Impossible were these goals of mine;
Doubt shackled my legs and duty chained
my neck to look at my captor;
Dim was my light as my dream bled out.


Then the sun saw me,
"Patience", he whispers, as he melts my
Chains.
The moon grants me sleep
As Hades treats my wounds,
"Not yet", he croons.


In the morning I awake as Artemis clothes
Me in new robes and Athena kisses my
cheeks,
"Survivor!", they sing, and equip me with a
Weaponized heart.

I arise defiant;
My gaze gentle but wise,
Ready to fight and ready to love,
I wander unto the path before me
And begin
My quest


— Heroine

Wrinkled hands grip the life boat paddle,
Rowing to find land
Parched and aged, I struggle to find home;
Too many storms have weathered my body
to a hollowed shell;


Desperate, I search for life
A siren calls my name ;
Her voice sings sweet lyrics proclaiming
freedom;
Doubtful I draw back, cautious of her lies;
Hopeful I lean in and she pulls me into the
waves
Into a deadly baptism


It is silent and bright;
I open my eyes and wipe the dust away;
Serenity leads me into the depths
As my corpse sails into the sun


In Atlantis, I transform;
I breathe with new ease
And sing with a strength I never knew;
In the water I glide untethered and
Fly with euphoric glow
And live for the first time

Deeper and deeper we dive into the shadows
And further and further I go;
Never to return again

— Cursed

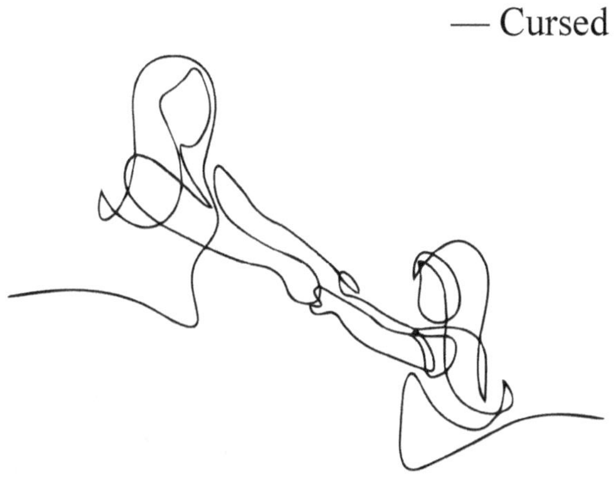

I shift into change and yet am the same.
The more I've learned,
The more unblind I've become
To the presence of the unknown;
A beast I cannot fully tame;

— Growth.